The Power Of Circles

The Design & Facilitation Of Engagement
Where We Learn, Work & Live

2014 Jack Ricchiuto
DesigningLife Books

Books by Jack Ricchiuto

Collaborative Creativity / 1996

Accidental Conversations / 2002

Project Zen / 2003

Appreciative Leadership / 2005

Mountain Paths / 2007

Conscious Becoming / 2008

Instructions From The Cook / 2009

The Stories That Connect You / 2010

The Enchantment Of Casual Origins / 2011

The Joy Of Thriving / 2012

Ordinary Eyes / 2012

The Agile Planning Field Guide / 2012

Abundant Possibilities / 2013

The Power Of Circles / 2014

The Power Of Circles
The Design & Facilitation Of Engagement
Where We Learn, Work & Live

Published by DesigningLife Books
1020 Kenilworth Avenue
Cleveland OH 44113 USA

ISBN 9781494928131 Paperback

First printing, January 2014
CreateSpace

Cover design: Tia Andrako

Contents

Invitation

I believe engagement will change the world. It already does.

Inspired by passion more than permission, we see people crafting their own learning portfolios, self-organizing their work and coming together to transform their communities.

Every week I meet more people in education, organizations and communities who believe that meaningful change will only come to the authentically engaged. They dream of a planet of engaged people wanting to make a difference. They have a passion for helping people take charge of their lives and their world.

I wrote this book for these visionaries who facilitate classes, courses, workshops, trainings, meetings, retreats, conference calls, videoconferencing, virtual work sessions, conferences, mediations, events, discussions, gatherings, planning efforts, design charrettes and collaborations.

Drawing from my decades of facilitating engagement and coaching and mentoring others in the craft, I outline the business case for engagement and a 5-dimensional model for the practice of facilitation.

The book offers 20 compelling principles toward a manifesto for engagement. It presents a handbook of 60 practice activities designed to help you develop the skillsets required to take your capacity for designing and facilitating engagement to new levels of impact.

You will discover how to animate and transform your learning, work and living environments as never before.

Jack Ricchiuto
October 2013

An engaged world

Imagine

Imagine a world in which people feel engaged where they learn, work and live. Envision a world where people come together to share responsibility for the character of their education, organizations and communities.

They decide what and how they will learn, contribute and connect in their world. They accept responsibility for their narratives rather than outsourcing them to others. They reclaim authorship of their common destinies.

In this world, we act empowered by the unprecedented abundance of knowledge and networks that continues to grow. We have access to more resources in one day than our grandparents had in an entire lifetime.

Until this era, we did not have the methodologies, technologies and science to make authentic and sustainable engagement possible. The many had to rely on a few to decide for them how they would learn, work and live.

The agrarian and industrial ages were dominated by a two-class system of power and responsibility haves and have-nots.

In the Information and Imagination Ages, the old system loses rigor and relevance. An infinite space of possibilities awaits those who discover they don't need other people to take responsibility for their world.

In the late 1970's, I began writing about the democratization of the workplace. It was not as much prescient of a dreamt future as descriptive of a profoundly shifting present.

Those of us mentored in facilitation were already self-organizing our development and performance in ways our decision makers couldn't or wouldn't.

With little faith in the validity of boundaries, we collaborated to achieve what no one could produce in isolation or competition.

We created our own learning and work plans. We transformed broken communities from the ground up.

Engagement makes sense in this era because every day, more challenges and opportunities require engaged people who become smarter together.

We have fewer of the simple problems that used to adequately get addressed by a hierarchy of individual decision makers. We no longer inhabit a planet populated with billions of people who want a privileged few to decide for them how they learn, work and live.

People don't want intermediaries and representatives. They want direct engagement empowered by their continuously evolving networks and technologies.

Engagement

We need a distinction for when people take and share responsibility for how things work in their world. I propose we use the possibility of engagement to narrate what happens when people share authorship for their experience where they learn, work and live.

In education, engaged students shape what and how they learn. In workplaces, people shape the technical and social character of their work. In communities, citizens shape the way they contribute to and benefit from the commons.

This profound shift from holding others responsible for us inspires and transforms. When you see people doing great and lovely things in ordinary or extraordinary ways, their attitude derives from engagement.

Engagement thrives in the realm of personal choice. We cannot force engagement, we can only facilitate it. We do not coerce it, we catalyze it.

In an engaged world, we still have people who act as stewards of resources and expertise. However, they don't diminish people's capacity for engagement by deciding for them how things work.

We now see more teachers, leaders and administrators interested in making the profound ontological shift from decision makers to facilitators because they feel deeply committed to growing a planet that flourishes with engaged people.

Decision making demystified

During a leadership workshop I facilitated some years ago, people waxed on about the primacy of leaders as decision makers.

The conversation shifted when a new supervisor raised an interesting and important question: Why would we expect that a peer promoted to a leadership position yesterday could make decisions today that merit our compliance?

What kind of overnight magic would need to occur to make that possible?

The question emerged in the era where information was only accessible to the elite members of closed meetings with other elites.

The question takes on a whole new twist in an era where, while the elite sequester themselves in meetings, people stay busy creating, archiving, accessing and sharing more information than their rookie or veteran decision makers could ever keep up with.

Students in education, employees in organizations and citizens in communities now enjoy access to more free apps and websites than they would ever need to manage all the real time and archived information from across the globe to make smart and timely decisions together.

As a result, engaged people self-organize and crowdsource their own solutions to problems and pathways to their dreams.

The decision makers more threatened than inspired by the democratization of information and knowledge actively and passively make these technologies less accessible and engagement less likely.

Contrary to all of this, engaged people can and will make decisions any single decision maker could make when they have the information necessary. Beyond that, we now know that decision making has higher quality when diverse perspectives contribute to the learning and creativity that go into good decision making.

In an engagement culture, we stop believing that any individuals could have more magical powers than a group could have.

We believe that, when we become engaged and informed, all of us become smarter than any one of us. This applies equally to decisions about degrees and curricula, organizational structure and performance and anything we could ever care about in our communities.

Engaged people make a difference.

The world you want to see

The commitment to engagement begins with a commitment to facilitation. Facilitation creates the space for people to co-create the world they want to see.

As facilitator, you want to engage people's gifts and passions. You want to see people come alive in their questions and become more in their collaborations. You want to make every conversation inclusive, inspiring and productive. You want to see people seamlessly move from uncertainty to discovery and from talk to action.

You want people to interact with trust, dream with courage, learn with curiosity and contribute with generosity because today's opportunities and problems require these.

You want to see people love change and thrive in differences. You want them to make timely and good decisions together. You want people to be driven by sustainably intrinsic rather than costly extrinsic motivators. You want to see them take initiative rather than wait to be managed.

Facilitation done well makes these possible in any context. It has been my experience over the past few decades that people show up when we design and facilitate spaces of engagement.

Facilitation works when we work from a belief that people will engage in spaces well-designed for that possibility.

Good facilitation works with what exists. It sails efficiently and successfully with whatever conditions and crew we have at hand.

We facilitate well because we draw from the core facilitation practices, principles, mindsets and skillsets that engage what we have in new ways to achieve new results.

In the power of facilitation as a creative process, like every creative process, we co-conspire with people to leverage what has been so far unengaged, underutilized and often unseen to do what some might even consider to be unlikely or impossible.

Facilitation realizes this dream. It happens every day around the world at the hands of engagement artisans. The more experience we have with facilitation, the less we become surprised by its power, yet always amazed and grateful for its possibility.

The power of circles

Engagement happens in circles. Figuratively and literally, circles express the essential spirit of engagement.

Most of what we enjoy today could never have come about through individual efforts alone. The best things in life come about when people do together what no one can do alone.

Serendipity ignites in the sparks of new intersections. Circles make the world go 'round.

When we invite engagement, we invite people to learn, work and connect their gifts together in circles. The evidence indicates that we learn better, work better and live better when we do it together.

When people feel divided they exercise a need for decision makers to deliver their survival. Connected people sculpt their own thrivancy. When it comes to unprecedented problems and opportunities, dialogue trumps compliance in the power of things that work.

We get more learned, done and shared in groups. Alignment accelerates learning, achieving and transformation.

We make long journeys together. We navigate a world of unprecedented change and complexity with unprecedented connectedness. This underscores why so many of the facilitation skillsets have to do with nurturing and leveraging new relationships.

Circles transcend the cultural divide between power and resource haves and have-nots. No one sits above or below others in circles. No one plays the role of head in the group's behalf. Circles remind us that each person's talents, stories and questions represent opportunity spaces.

When we become smarter together, all heads, hearts and hands matter.

Circles invite sharing. People share what they have to do what they can together. People help each other do whatever they're trying to do. In a circle, each contribution to the whole becomes a contribution to the parts.

Engaged people help each other learn, get things done, discover new resources, connect with new people in new ways and make the most of their least engaged resources and gifts. Everything occurs in a spirit of personalized mutual gain. Generosity replaces defensive competition driven by the intention to creates losers.

Circles work by invitation. We coerce no one to join or stay. People feel free to participate, contribute and collaborate. The more people feel coerced, the less engaged they think, feel and interact.

Engagement works in agile circles that expand and contract depending on the nature of the conversations and actions engaged.

Large groups get large things done in nested networks of smaller groups. With the simplest of technologies, circles can grow across geographies, sectors and disciplines.

Circles transcend the defensive and divisive boundaries of institutions more interested in narcissistic survival than the empowerment of people and new emergent wholes. Empowerment and engagement yet remain elusive metrics for many organizations and institutions.

We create circles of students and alumni, local businesses and specialized experts, researchers and funders, crowdsourcing entrepreneurs and early adopters, youth and mentors, parents and retirees, artists and landlords, grass roots organizers and volunteers. The possibilities have only the limits of imagination.

Facilitation makes circles more possible and more powerful.

The engagement imperative

Since the beginnings of my career as engagement artisan in the 1970s I've guided people in learning how to act and feel engaged.

I've worked with some of the most passionate and amazing people on the planet. I've spent fruitful days in schools and colleges, hospitals and non-profits, corporations and startups, communities and networks.

I've designed and facilitated engagement in groups of a few to hundreds. I've worked in contexts of peace and violence, stability and turmoil, transition and transformation, fragmentation and fermentation.

I have seen people come alive as never before when we empower and facilitate their engagement. I have seen engagement transform people and the contexts in which they strive and thrive.

Every group on the planet contains people passionate about engagement. Their demographics of geography, gender and generation do not define or confine their passion for engagement. They want to bring out their best and bring out the best in others. They want engagement in their schools, organizations and communities.

They believe that people realize the metrics of collective well-being to the extent that they actively engage everyone's best. Even without knowing the research that supports this, they believe that engaged people create, connect and contribute far more than than their unengaged peers.

Consider the current trends in urban renaissance, the transitions to democratic societies, the empowerment of women, the revitalization of entrepreneurship and the proliferation of technologies that raise the quality of living across the planet.

All of these originate from engaged people, people with little interest in compliance or resistance, people who refuse to wait to be invited to make the impossible just a little more possible.

We now see entrepreneurs come together to innovate what big companies and institutions don't dare. We see students come together to help each other learn what they don't learn in class. We see employees launch new enterprises that invigorate local living economies.

New networks emerge daily where people share spaces, cars, bicycles, couches, tools, seeds, dreams and anything that they can.

These trends stretch back to the beginning of human history. Students always got their best learning done in circles of peers. Economies always transformed from the unpredictable convergences of engaged people with entrepreneurial spirits.

We see people in neighborhoods coming together to do what their cities do not. Cities do what states do not. States, provinces and regions do what countries do not. Engagement makes the difference: people taking rather than delegating responsibility for their common destinies and legacies.

The engagement distinction

As facilitators, we work from a distinction between engagement and participation. Although we can design any event or process as a hybrid of participation and engagement, we do not confuse the two.

In participation, people comply with the wishes of decision makers. They participate in what others decide for them.

They participate in classes and courses, work and project teams, community groups and events others define and direct. They follow what others determine.

Decision makers assess participants on their capacity for compliance. They confer extrinsic rewards on compliant students, employees, customers and citizens who follow rather than question directives.

Participation turns into engagement the instant we take people's questions seriously, using them to help shape the opportunity spaces they share.

Participation does not represent a problem. It can make good things happen. It can result from good decision making or good facilitation.

Many of the facilitator skillsets work equally well in participation or engagement contexts. The facilitation of engagement requires a whole additional alchemy of skillsets because of the qualitative differences between engagement and participation.

Engagement contrasts with participation in that in engagement, we facilitate a group's decisions about how they will interact rather than decide for them.

As facilitators, we create interesting and compelling experiences and spaces that liberate people to take responsibility for what they learn, create, test, build and celebrate.

We do not take responsibility away by acting as decision makers for a group. We guide people to successfully learn how to take responsibility for their experience.

When we work from an intention of engagement, we measure our success by how much of a sense of ownership people feel for what they do and achieve together.

Eulogy for the old model

We move on from the old decision maker model with a proper eulogy.

The decision maker model brought us the industrial era with its promise of better lives. It took education and religion to scale. It created expansive institutions of culture, science, technology, entertainment and government and fueled the colonistic regimes that built mass empires, mass production and mass consumption.

Generations later, we still have people who cannot imagine a world without decision makers. The demand for decision makers derives its gravitas from a mythological fear that without them, we would all get helplessly sucked into downward spirals of anarchy and chaos.

When people have good facilitators or can facilitate themselves well, they don't need decision makers. Faith replaces fear and people discover the grace of empowered connectivity.

Facilitating engagement creates more authentic caring and belonging than a culture of decision makers could ever mandate.

We now live in an amazing opportunity space of empowerment. We have teachers, leaders and administrators who want this new world of engagement.

They have curiously moved on from holding to sharing power. They have become facilitators instead of decision makers.

They discover that people can quickly become equipped and empowered to share responsibility for decisions.

They more and more realize that no teacher or trainer could ever personally deliver what anyone can now access with a charged phone. No leader or administrator could personally know or keep up with what a connected group could. No decision maker could personally have more data than a group of curious data curators.

The world has grown far too complex and dynamic for any group to depend on decision makers especially when the new technologies and sociologies empower people otherwise.

Pushback on the pushback

Everyone has stories of groups failing to be productive, whether the examples feature a group of students in education, employees in organizations or citizens in communities.

A decision maker delegates some task, problem or assignment to a group that fails to produce efficient and successful results.

None of this equates to empirical evidence that without a decision maker, groups have no hope of doing well in whatever they strive to do. It does speak to the fact that without good facilitation, groups struggle.

When they struggle, groups of unengaged people inaccurately assign blame to decision maker, resource, personality or influence deficiencies.

From a facilitator mindset, we see group success and failure as a design and facilitation issue. We believe groups do well when we or they skillfully design and facilitate their process.

Even without perceived adequate resources, personalities and influence, engaged groups achieve more than what could be achieved by any one person, including even the most celebrated and charismatic decision makers.

Struggling groups do not need more decision makers taking responsibility away from them. They thrive with facilitation that empowers and equips them for success.

Facilitating for engagement requires different skillsets than decision making for compliance.

The role of decision maker demands the skillsets of imposition, inspection, instruction, interference and incentivizing. Facilitation requires the skillsets of inquiry, intuition, intention, influence and improvisation.

When we intend engagement, we create the kinds of questions, suggestions and experiences that get people discovering their potentials. We make it more possible for people to realize a faith in themselves that energizes them to do just about anything they put their minds, hearts and hands to.

What engagement looks like

When I facilitate groups, I draw from dozens of models and principles, I offer them just in time when I feel the group would most benefit from them.

To stay true to an intention of authentic engagement, I leave the nature of the path to the group's responsibility. When I take responsibility away from a group, I cease to facilitate and turn into a decision maker. Engagement turns into participation.

When we engage people, we remove the artificial boundaries of learning, working and connecting. We don't fragment learning to education, work to organizations or connecting to communities.

We integrate work and connecting into learning, learning into work and connecting and connecting into work and learning. We remove the walls between each space of intention.

People share responsibility for creating the questions, agreements and conversations that guide them in their efforts. Those assigned as teachers, leaders and administrators design and facilitate this.

The ultimate expression of engagement occurs in the design and empowerment of self-organizing groups at whatever level and function they perform. Self-organizing groups outperform decision maker dependent groups by several factors.

Engaged people show up

As we move toward a more engaged society, this effort will take on a variety of forms, some of which we cannot even predict.

At all levels of education, learners create their own learning portfolios. Actual projects, internships, volunteering and work provide live contexts for learning, even at earlier grade levels.

Gardening and culinary projects that serve a community or organization can empower learning all the basics of reading, writing, math, science, history, health, civics, sociology and the arts. Building, repair and entrepreneurship projects engage higher levels of learning through creativity and critical thinking.

In organizations, people can cross-learn many skillsets across functions, leading to more agility and flexibility during times of change. People schedule, organize and plan their own work, communication and quality assurances.

Well-facilitated, people act proactively, strategically and collaboratively within and between functions. They shape their continuous learning and learning of the organization.

In communities, people create their own local economies of barter and volunteering. They self-organize events, celebrations and festivals. They actively offer support and resources to entrepreneurial startups and pop-ups.

People form associations and networks that share responsibility for basics like gardens and farms, all forms of repair and preventive safety. They participate in crowd-sourced public service and leadership transparencies.

In each case, facilitation makes it easier for people to shape how things look, feel and work. We now have the sociology and technology to give facilitation the power to enable engagement.

Facilitation creates the space for engagement. Facilitation creates a culture of responsibility, resourcefulness and relationships.

When they no longer get distracted by the constraints of compliance, people act with courage, creativity, connectivity, curiosity and compassion.

When we bring out our best

When facilitation brings out their best, people instinctively figure out how to learn, work and live well together.

Without the extrinsic standards and incentives of decision makers, people all over the world daily engage their best in doing what no single decision maker has the skill or will to achieve.

When people bring out their best, they accomplish amazing things. They transform villages and neighborhoods. They self-organize all kinds of new learning and multiple career shifts.

They co-invent breakthroughs within and across industry and discipline sectors. They work in global networks to innovate beyond what their sponsor companies have achieved.

For disengagement to exist, it must be specifically designed into the shape of our education systems, organizations and institutions.

In most situations where we see local and global problems persist, we see unengaged people.

We see employers hire graduates unprepared for work and careers. We see organizations with shorter life spans than people who make less than two dollars a day. We see people go whole lifetimes entirely unconscious of the rich gifts and dreams of their neighbors.

All of this happens in the transition from decision makers to facilitators.

The state of engagement

According to current research, the majority of students in education, employees at work and citizens in communities feel disengaged. In many cases it exceeds 70% across contexts.

Decision maker centered institutions and organizations don't even measure for engagement, so it doesn't even have a chance for legitimization or development. Hitting one's numbers does not guarantee a valid metric for engagement levels.

In the old model, we talk about good students as compliant consumers and producers. We talk about good employees and citizens in the same vein.

At the inflection point where available knowledge makes people smarter together than their decision makers, decision maker superiority not only loses relevance but becomes the ultimate direct cause of disengagement.

Education systems still measure and incentivize students on how much knowledge they consume to produce test scores.

Organizations still measure and incentivize workers on how well they consume raw materials to produce consumers of finished goods and services.

Communities still measure and incentivize citizenship on how much they consume from the community's businesses and institutions to produce security and debt.

In the old culture, we equate consumption and production with engagement. The more people consume and produce what decision makers mandate and regulate, the more we considered them engaged.

The equation speaks to an unsustainable denial of people's gifts. In engagement, people use their gifts to decide together the form, feel and function of their world.

In an engagement culture, students co-design how they learn what they learn. Employees co-design how they produce what they produce. Citizens co-design how they share their gifts for a commons of well-being.

People in positions of teaching, leading and organizing facilitate engagement in these contexts. Each context measures success in terms of the scope and depth of engagement.

Engaged people feel abundant. The feeling of abundance derives from a contributor identity. People feel chronically deficient in a consumer identity. The happiness research bears this out. Givers experience 3-5 times more happiness than receivers.

The transition

The transition from decision maker to facilitator requires three core elements: education, empowerment and experimentation.

People used to the role of decision maker must learn why engagement creates flourishing schools, workplaces and communities.

They must be empowered with permission and new skillsets to shift responsibility to students, employees and citizens. They must experiment in the art and science of designing and facilitating engagement.

A sustainable transition will occur organically, one step at a time. Early adopter schools, organizations and communities will lead the way. Others will follow when they feel they can trust the legitimacy, possibility and power of facilitating engagement.

Some decision makers will initially refuse to consider facilitation. They will refuse education, empowerment and experimentation. Some will join later.

Regardless of the adoption rates toward facilitating engagement, more people will embrace and contribute to a growing culture of engagement.

We will see more entrepreneurs defining leadership for their new enterprises in terms of facilitation rather than decision makers. We will see people in communities launching and crowdsourcing their own engaged alternatives to anything established business, institutions and school fail to innovate.

We will see more people forming their own schools, their own career learning portfolios, their own projects and enterprises.

People will flourish in the emergence and evolution of sharing economies, crowdsourced funding and grass roots transformations. All of this will occur because of the growth of engagement.

People who invest time to develop their facilitation capacities will feel a sense of social responsibility for doing so. They will transform how people learn, work and live.

Practices of facilitation

The why of facilitation

Until people become adept at facilitating their own engagement together, engagement requires skillful facilitation.

Without good facilitation, people unaccustomed to engagement get stuck. They don't sync together, they produce more talk than action and the experience does not exactly qualify as a source of happiness. They feel inadequate without strong decision makers.

People act at odds with each other. They operate more from personalities than agreements. Those who feel superior blame their perceived inferior peers for frustrations and disappointments.

They don't bring out their best and the best in each other. They remain unproductively self-reliant, defensive and competitive instead of resourceful, creative and collaborative.

Interestingly, all of these can just as easily happen when decision makers manage groups.

All of these simply indicate people's unfamiliarity with engagement. Everyone has the basic skills required for their engagement. Facilitation draws from these skills to make engagement possible.

Anyone can learn how to facilitate engagement well. By the time we're around eight years old, we have the basic skills necessary to develop the facilitation mindsets and skillsets.

These basic skills include things like inquiry, empathy, listening, research, connecting, improvisation and storytelling. These provide the essential ingredients for a lifetime of cooking up interesting and compelling engagement experiences.

The five practices of facilitation

We think of facilitation as the alchemy of five core practices: noticing, nurturing, knitting, noodling and nudging. This 5-dimensional model serves as a simple recipe for an incredibly rich craft.

We notice what kinds of knowledge and abilities people bring to the table. Using our attention, intuition and questions, we pay attention to how people connect and get stuck.

Noticing empowers us to create a safe space for risk taking, connect people in new ways, spark new possibilities and help people engage their strengths.

We nurture a culture of belonging, hospitality and trust. These support a group's willingness to listen, inquire and explore new vistas.

Nurturing empowers people to view their differences as gifts to engage rather than problems to fix. When people feel valued, they feel a passion to deepen and extend their potentials.

We knit new connections among people within and beyond a group. The quality of a group's performance depends on the quality of its interactions.

Connected people learn and do more together. They act with more courage than fear, giving them an agile and proactive resilience.

We noodle with a group on new ways to get anything done. We foster new options and alternatives. We guide people in how to grow creative possibilities together.

We encourage people to treat everything they do as an experiment so reflected experience becomes an empowering guide in their success.

We nudge people beyond their familiarity boundaries. We nudge with new questions, suggestions and stories. Our nudging infuses people with a contagious confidence that empowers them to try new things.

We encourage them to do what they can without permission or approval. We help them surprise even themselves with great things.

Facilitation as design

Facilitators think as designers.

We design local and virtual spaces, conversations and discoveries. We design ways for people to do research and experiments, sharing and collaborating.

At the heart of facilitating engagement, we design ways for people to experience the kinds of relationships that make engagement possible.

Engagement requires peer relationships of empathy and respect, trust and resilience. We now know how to help people productively leverage the diversity of personalities and perspectives.

As no era before us, we have compelling and adaptive models to create new synergies of gifts. We remain committed to growing the boundless art and science of relationships that empower the possibilities of engagement.

Equipped with the five dimensions of facilitation, we make it easier for people to quickly and sustainably come together as never before.

Noticing

Every detail and pattern we notice about any group becomes meaningful to the design and facilitation of their engagement. We make it our business to know any group better than it might know itself.

Change remains the constant in groups. Facilitation works when we pay continuous attention to whatever emerges and shifts in how people feel, think and interact.

We use all of our senses and intuition to form impressions. We listen to how we feel as a barometer of what's happening below the surface. Intuition plays a key part in this.

We notice patterns of interaction, eye contact and emotional energy. We notice what people freely talk about and what seems obviously not talked about, things unconsidered or undiscussable.

The more we practice intuition, the more we can sense in groups what might not reveal itself as evident. Noticing shifts in the group reveals new opportunities for nurturing, knitting, noodling and nudging.

Noticing has power because it goes beyond assumptions. We check everything out with people. We test every hunch and inquire into every sense we have about the group. We test for interest, readiness and willingness. We don't rely on history, common sense or the opinions of others.

In facilitation, we work with the group we have, never with the group we imagine, hope or think we have. We work with their gifts and feelings, relationships and questions. It all begins with noticing.

Nurturing

People engage their gifts in new ways when they feel supported and safe to do so.

Support validates the legitimacy of their experience. It doesn't remove inevitable uncertainties but provides a safe space for people to try new ways of thinking, learning, interacting and growing.

How far people stretch their potentials depends on how much support they feel to do so.

We provide affirmation for people's experience as well as invite people to provide peer support in the group. People act with more courage when they feel trust of the group in which they feel engaged.

Trusts also forms from agreements. We facilitate the group's experimenting with agreements on how things happen, get done and communicated.

Groups that work by mutual agreement work by design. Working by design acts as the functional alternative to working by dictate, dominating personalities or default. People support what they help create.

Validating the truth of people's experience neither agrees nor disagrees with another's feelings, stories or dreams. It simply acknowledges the truth of what people feel. Validation empathizes with the reality of their happiness or misery.

It creates a kind of listening where people do not feel alone. When people feel connected, they engage their gifts with a greater sense of generosity and flexibility.

Knitting

Connected people become unstoppable. We continuously discover and invent new ways to connect people in whatever they're about and doing.

We connect them as they do learning, working and coming together in the commons. We work to challenge myths about self-reliance that deny the power of collaboration.

People learn, work and live better in a rich ecology of relationships both inside and beyond the groups they participate in. Our relationships extend the horizons of our potentials.

We get people discovering each other's questions, stories and gifts so they can help each other more fluidly and regularly. We design new collaborations to connect people across the chasms of cliques and clusters.

We invite new conversations that convene people from the cores and peripheries of networks and communities.

We help people discover the potential power of their commonalities and complements across contexts of different perspectives, politics and dreams.

We use storytelling to deepen bonds so resonance supports new efforts at connecting and reconnecting where trust hasn't yet developed or needs to be restored. Stories have a unique power to connect people in resonant feelings and identities.

The more connected people feel, the more they share what they know, who they know and what they have to offer.

Part of our work as facilitator helps people discover that in a world of unprecedented change and connectivity, who we know becomes as important, if not more important, than what we know.

We measure part of our significance as facilitator in measures of how many new useful relationships people cultivate because of our knitting.

Noodling

In noodling with a group, we invite planned and unplanned improvisation, experimentation and creativity. We model and engage people in tinkering with new resources, approaches, models and variations on themes. We improvise new experiences to facilitate new discoveries.

We do this with new ways of learning, doing and sharing together. Noodling can give vitality to what has so far been a source of uninspired tedium.

New habits can be invented, tested and improvised. New agreements can replace ones that haven't quite worked well for everyone in enough situations.

We noodle on how to find new resources, how to package or present something in a fresh way. We noodle on new and better ways to communicate stories achieved and lessons learned. We noodle on different models of planning, organizing and critiquing work.

As facilitators, we model and invite noodling. We use our own ideas and questions to spark and jump start any group's creative process.

We bring in and encourage sharing interesting new examples of creativity, innovation and entrepreneurship locally and globally. We draw as much inspiration from outside the group as possible.

Nudging

Nudging gently leans people into the directions of their potentials. At the core of nudging, we ask all kinds of questions that invite people into new distinctions and considerations, conversations and actions.

In contrast to nudging, we lecture. Distracted from humility, we impose our opinions under the guise that we know better than the group, which might be true, but in facilitation this becomes irrelevant.

We nudge with questions. Our vocabulary of inquiry extends across the whole spectrum of who, what, when, where, why, how, how much, how fast, which and what if.

Through a rich improvisation of questions, we move people into new spaces of thinking, learning, imagining, inquiring, connecting, doing and behaving. We use questions to turn walls into windows and windows into doors.

We help people discover where they don't even need permission to pursue new possibilities. Questions inspire courage. They empower people. They speak to the part of us that yearns for new horizons.

The engagement manifesto

To an engaged world

Designing and facilitating engagement requires a whole different mindset from what many of us might be accustomed. We express this mindset in a manifesto of principles. These 20 principles outline how we think as we shape experiences that create space for engagement.

1.   We move in the direction of our conversations
2.   Engagement focuses on gifts
3.   Success inspires success
4.   Engagement requires facilitation
5.   We support what we help create
6.   Thriving workplaces engage
7.   Engaged communities care
8.   Subject matter experts have power as peers
9.   We use the skills available
10.   In our best learning we learn how to learn
11.   Interested people get and stay engaged
12.   We make fear optional
13.   Facilitators refuse to take away responsibility
14.   We liberate people with social technologies
15.   Engagement requires new funding models
16.   We make engagement a movement
17.   Our engagement facilitates engagement
18.   Social capital rules
19.   Engagement has no borders
20.   Narratives trump numbers

1. We move in the direction of our conversations

We define engagement as conversations of commitment about how things work. When people have these conversations, they feel engaged. People who feel engaged act engaged.

The research across contexts clearly indicates that engaged people interact with more creativity and collaboration, courage and resilience, passion and generosity.

They learn faster and more sustainably. They thrive on new challenges and change. They share more of their time and talents for the well-being of the commons.

2. Engagement focuses on gifts

Everyone has gifts. Our gifts come in the form of talents, resources, knowledge, stories and questions. Everyone also has weaknesses: things we don't do well or consistently.

When we facilitate engagement, we start with what people have that has value to themselves and others. We focus on these. We take time to discover, talk about, offer and invite them.

The compliance model focuses on weaknesses. The operating principle argues, without empirical evidence, that getting people to do their best requires auditing, editing and deleting weaknesses.

The engagement model works from the evidence that we realize our potentials to the extent that we engage our gifts in ways that make our weaknesses less relevant.

People who initiate and innovate the most amazing changes in the world do so with as many weaknesses as everyone else. Their stories represent testaments to what happens when we sustain passionate and productive focus on engaging our gifts.

They work magic with what they have instead of trying to do something with what they lack. They work from an abundance rather than deficiency model.

Some people resist this possibility. They cannot bring themselves to believe that focusing on gifts works. Their learned beliefs deny the feasibility. They feel genuinely and inconsolably anxious not talking about and fixing weaknesses.

The idea that people have everything they need to do something new feels foreign even though no data legitimizes a focus on weaknesses.

Facilitation empowers people because it focuses on gifts. This builds the confidence people need to try new ways of learning, working and connecting.

3. Success inspires success

For the same reasons facilitation focuses on gifts, it also focuses on success. The more successful people feel, the more success they seek and the more capable they feel of it.

The culture of compliance pays lip service to success, obsessing more with the analysis of failure, disappointment and blame. When people improve, they do so in spite of any focus on failure.

People feel disengaged when they feel inadequate. They come alive in celebration of their ability to succeed, even and especially with small successes.

We fail most profoundly when we fail to learn from our successes. We use and replicate success only when we learn from it. Every minute of focusing on failure postpones learning from successes.

In facilitating engagement, we invite people to reflect deeply and accurately on the causes of whatever they do that works. Their experience becomes their most powerful teacher. They learn to rely on their own wisdom which makes their leaning sustainable and portable.

When we realistically examine failure, we discover that failure often comes from failing to engage our best.

We engage our gifts to the extent that we sustain consciousness of them. Nothing has more power to remind us of our gifts than focusing on our successes of any size or shape.

Every person and group on the planet does something right every day. Everyone does something that works. Everyone achieves something of value in spite of the odds otherwise.

Engagement begins with this acknowledgment. No one can be engaged unless they understand their successes and gifts. Facilitation makes this possible.

4. Engagement requires facilitation

Many people find engagement odd. It represents an unusual and unexpected way of interacting. People acquiesce to disengagement because of its normative precedence.

In business as usual, people expect to follow the directives of decision makers. Engagement invites them to take responsibility for their own experience.

Facilitation makes this possible. Facilitation gives people the tools to act empowered, think of themselves as empowered and feel empowered. Without facilitation, people feel largely powerless, giving away their power to whoever has the position to claim it.

People used to disengagement do not naturally feel and act engaged until we facilitate them to do so. No amount

of intimidation or incentives can substitute for the power
of facilitation.

5. We support what we help create

Compliance often requires extrinsic motivators because
people do not necessarily have personal or sustainable
passion for what compliance requires.

People do not naturally support what others dictate or
mandate. They support what they help create. They act
with authentic, natural and personal commitment to what
they help decide.

It takes sufficient incentives or threats for people to follow
through on things they don't create. Compliance creates
more direct and indirect costs than engagement.

When people decide together on what they want to do,
their intrinsic motivation does not require the expense of
motivational substitutes.

Engaged students who structure their learning based on
their questions relentlessly pursue their leaning with
passion. Co-workers who cooperatively feel like co-
owners in their organizations become innovators.

Community members who crowdsource business and
personal loan and barter structures, home schooling
coops, local food systems, pop up events and festivals

volunteer more time and talent than anyone knew could
be available.

6. Thriving workplaces engage

In engaged workplaces, people decide together how best
to listen to their customers in producing deliverables and
brands that work. They design their own performance
assessment, orientation and development models.

They create agreements on how work gets done, how
things get communicated and how best to leverage
everyone's gifts, passions and interests. They decide how
best to use the full range of technologies to make things
easier and everyone more accessible.

They collaborate to improve and innovate, think like
entrepreneurs and deliver value to their customers and
stakeholders. They develop strategic directions and
projects to make the organization proactive and agile in
its markets.

Leaders act as facilitators to help people have the
conversations that make these forms of engagement
possible. Facilitators build and leverage their social equity
and informal influence to keep obstacles clear so people
can do their individual and collective best.

They connect dots to build the kinds of trust relationships
that make courage, creativity and collaboration possible.

They help people see differences as pathways rather than problems.

The research indicates that when we engage people they outperform the unengaged by wide margins and their organizations outperform others across metrics. The compliance of the unengaged pales in return on investment comparisons.

7. Engaged communities care

In a culture of engagement, people take charge of their neighborhoods and networks. They form new collaborations and projects that do what their institutions and social programs fall short on because of skill, will and resource constraints.

Institutional, community and grassroots leaders and network weavers act as facilitators to these efforts.

Engaged people crowdsource resident information, knowledge, experience and expertise to communicate new problems, changes, updates, solutions, alternatives and resources. They collectively understand issues, challenges and opportunities in ways that no longer require the bottlenecks of decision makers.

They create agreements called policies, ordinances and standards that they feel a sense of authorship over and therefore more supportive about.

Facilitation weaves new networks of sharing gifts, opportunities and dreams enabling people to do together the perceived impossible. We help people feel permission to discover and do what they used to postpone in a culture of compliance.

Sustainable communities with strong quality of life and well-being indicators will come about through more engaged citizens. The transition to facilitated engagement makes this possible.

8. Subject matter experts have power as peers

The complexity of life and work will continue to require subject matter experts in every field, endeavor and discipline. These specialists give depth to learning, research, design and development.

As facilitators, we need subject matter expertise in the design and facilitation of engagement. We don't necessarily need to have the subject matter expertise related to whatever people engage in.

I have successfully facilitated projects with people across industries doing work in which I had no subject matter expertise. Good facilitators can facilitate anything.

We simply need to notice when a group needs to engage a subject matter expert into the conversation.

We spend time helping the group prepare and use the expert well. We help them develop good questions and applications of expertise received. We don't expect experts will necessarily know what people need or want to know and do. Many do not have expertise in facilitation as well.

We don't position any expert as knowing better than the group what it needs to do. Good facilitation enables the group to wisely use all of their resources. The more self-organizing people become in their engagement, the more we can trust them to know what's best for their well-being individually and collectively.

As facilitators, we connect dots of expertise and use. We help people engage experts just in time when they need it. We keep building our network of experts who can be available to the group's continuous learning.

9. We use the skills available

Engaged groups interact with skills and skillsets we don't observe with unengaged groups.

They interact with curiosity and empathy. They ask for and offer help. They share resources, decisions and opportunities. They take small steps toward big dreams. They take initiative. They act with transparency and trustworthiness. They celebrate progress.

These skills reside in most everyone on the planet. They don't have to be learned or taught, only invited and engaged. They exist alongside whatever personality labels we place on people.

These skills become available to the degree people feel responsible for their experience. They exist but become less accessible to groups that don't take and share responsibility for how they learn, work and live.

People derive intrinsic happiness whenever we call on these skills. Facilitation evokes this possibility.

10. In our best learning we learn how to learn

Old industrial models of education measured success as the mass production of diplomas, certificates and degrees. That was in an era where we could fairly accurately predict what people would need to know for their future work and careers.

It was a time when the predictability of social roles and work required only that schools teach people how to be dependent consumers of knowledge instead of self-organizing co-creators of learning.

The engagement model measures success as the cultivation of passionate learners. Passionate learners know how to manage their own learning in any context, especially in the growing unpredictability of future contexts.

Passionate learners shape the learning curves of their own alternative credentials, startup enterprises, sustainable practices and personal growth programs. They onboard into organizations as fast learners. Their capacity for self-directed learning makes them resilient surfers of change.

Now that students have unlimited access to what they can learn, it becomes more relevant that education teaches people how to learn. How to passively memorize anything that's already on a screen has nothing to do with learning how to learn. This represents learning what to learn.

People who learn how to learn can translate all manner of uncertainties into questions that access new resources for real world applications. Facilitation makes this possible.

In a culture of facilitated education, people base their learning on their own evolving questions. They develop all new learning in ways that engage their passions and interests. They locate and use their own resources, using each other, browsers and subject matter experts as sources and guides.

They develop their own portfolios and projects to demonstrate their new learning. They organize how to collaborate in projects and portfolios. They create agreements on how they will behave and interact, communicate and coordinate with each other throughout.

Facilitators act as subject matter experts and connect learners to other experts in the community and beyond.

Technology figures prominently in everything. We connect learners to the endlessly accessible and valid learning resources online and virtually.

All of these new engagement competences enable and empower learners to have amazing career resiliency in an era where the character of work will continue to change unpredictably. Learners who have experienced engaged learning will be the ones who thrive.

11. Interested people get and stay engaged

Facilitation asks people about their interests.

We ask students what they want to learn and help others learn. We ask employees what they want to do and help others do. We ask community members what they want to share and help others share.

We don't micromanage their answers. We don't tell them what to think or decide. We leave it up to them. They get better at this with reflected experience. We trust passion to engage strengths into relevant value. We have faith in their unique interests.

We listen deeply to what people want to do and help them learn that, do that and contribute that.

We have incredible faith in the power of curiosity. We trust people's questions. We believe people will do great things simply from the continuous evolution of inquiry that shapes and inspires any journey.

The magic of engagement inspires this alchemy in new chemistries of curiosity.

12. We make fear optional

Fear debilitates us from engagement.

We use fear to protect ourselves from failure. The vicious cycle of fear prevents us from trying anything new, and in so doing, prevents us from discovering new forms of success. In a classic self-defeating, self-fulfilling prediction, we try nothing new and get nothing new.

As facilitators, we stay sensitive and empathetic to this dynamic. We know our own fears and their seductive lies.

The more intolerable failure becomes, the more fear becomes a compelling excuse for a disengaged life.

In our work as facilitators, we help people do new things with uncertain outcomes. We do this by continuously reminding them they already have all the prerequisite skills to try them out.

We layer one level of success after another in small, organic and iterative steps. Each step creates the confident energy to propel people to and through the next step.

People disable themselves by trying to take on too much at once instead of minimizing risks working one small step at a time. They incorrectly assume they must know how to proceed in order to proceed. They lack familiarity with trusted guides.

Ultimately they discover their own inner trusted guides and venture into new landscapes they would never had dreamed possible.

We offer no false feedback. We name mistakes quickly, cleanly and instructively. Every vibration of confidence comes from authentic acknowledgement of gifts and celebrations of progress.

With experience, people become at first less paralyzed by uncertainty and eventually energized and inspired by it. New levels of engagement become possible.

13. Facilitators refuse to take away responsibility

Engagement creates people who self-organize. They release unnecessary dependencies on decision makers. Decision makers who have unique subject matter expertise and relational influence instead become liberated to provide these kinds of value when needed.

Self-organizing people dream bigger, contribute more, connect more and enjoy their learning, work and life more. They guide their own learning, working and living.

Even though we can do things for others as facilitators, we empower and equip them to do those for themselves. This includes defining the direction of their engagement in learning, work and collaborating.

We have to get over the narcissistic mythology that our role, intelligence or experience anoint us with special powers unavailable to others.

Before we had the neuroscience and technologies to democratize learning, the hypnosis about the superiority of decision makers was a compelling and irresistible meme.

We have to live in the real world of current time where people can learn to be individually and collectively self-organizing. They can take responsibility for their health and well-being, growth and contributions. They can create and take on work that serves the intersection of societal value and vocational passions. They can take responsibility for life long learning.

This transformation has two requirements: we learn to become facilitators and we stay out of the way of people's self-organizing capabilities.

Staying out of the way does not mean withholding our gifts. It means making them immediately available, just in time, when people invite them. It means offering our gifts when we know they have the potential to add value to people's self-organizing pursuits.

It means never taking responsibility away from people just because we think our job requires it or that we think we must for their own good.

Not taking responsibility away from people, but instead helping people discover the possibility of taking it for themselves, remains our sacred vow as facilitators. We honor and legitimize the validity of engaged others.

Only when people feel completely responsible for their experience do they begin to act accordingly. Only facilitation has the power to make this possible when people have been accustomed otherwise.

14. We liberate people with social technologies

Social technologies crowdsource knowledge and information. They tell people the best ways to navigate, shop locally, transfer talents, pool resources, work together on common issues, pursue together common dreams.

As we head toward a planet of people virtually connected, we make it more possible for people to do what no school, institution, company, industry or discipline can do within its walls.

When we connect the dots of knowledge and information, we connect people in knowing how to create thriving regions and cities.

We already have all of the free collaborative tools we need to make all of this happen and this space grows daily and exponentially.

As facilitators, we help people learn how to use new tools to do together what can only be done together. We expand their imaginations to embrace possibilities that call them into circles of greater aliveness.

15. Engagement requires new funding models

To move engagement forward, we no longer rely on old funding models. We change how we fund innovation, entrepreneurship and change.

The old models funded compliance, consumption and competition.

In a world committed to engagement, funders empower and equip fundees to empower and equip the people they serve.

The new metrics of engagement feature a bias for collaboration. Instead of funding old competitions, we fund new collaborations. We fund for rhyzomic impacts. This expectation requires fundees to use parts of their funds to start up like efforts and enterprises. This scales engagement.

16. We make engagement a movement

For engagement to grow, it cannot be relegated to an elite few. It must become a movement.

It needs to be accessible in all corners of the world, to people with and without economic security. It remains the promise of the many, the inheritance of all without exception.

To do this, we need to grow boundaryless networks of facilitators, people skilled in knowing how to notice, nurture, knit, noodle and nudge.

We need them in classrooms and courses, onsite and online. We need them in the teams and organizations, in the formal and informal groups in communities.

Engagement will grow at the pace and scale we grow facilitators empowering people with new capabilities in engagement.

As more decision makers discover the power of facilitation, the more they will sponsor, support and fund the growth of facilitators in every imaginable context.

17. Our own engagement facilitates engagement

Authentic facilitators earn credibility in the stories of their own engagement. They inspire by showing more than telling.

As facilitators, we walk the talk. We have no faith in lip service to engagement. We do not ask people to act more engaged in their world than we act engaged in ours.

We do not express surprise when people take charge of their world and lives.

We expect to hear and tell countless stories each year of people emerging from the edges with brilliant spirits of courage and ingenuity.

We live lives of seamless improvisation. We take responsibility for our learning, growing, contributing and participating. We cultivate and share rich ecologies of resources.

We treat all strangers as brothers and sisters in the family of life. We treat the earth as our body, the sky as our spirit and the water as our mother.

We ply our craft of facilitation in a global guild of engagement.

18. Social capital rules

In a world of unprecedented change and connectedness, who we know becomes as important as what we know.

This possibility takes on new significance in a world where we live less than a dozen steps from billions of people with an abundant diversity of gifts.

Facilitation removes boundaries in new connections.

We connect students to people in the community who can share knowledge, skillsets and wisdom. We connect people in workplaces searching for new ideas with people around the world who have them. We connect people and opportunities in communities to others with diverse resources.

We connect people and nurture the connections by helping them initiate concrete actions to build trust and resonance. We refuse to be the sage on their stage that preempts their capacity for building the social capital of new connections.

We encourage them to use any media and means available. We help them view the people they know as potential connectors to those they don't.

We empower them to discover the abundant world awaiting them just beyond the horizons of the familiar.

19. Engagement has no borders

The geopolitical landscape today struggles in crisis. We still have national and state leaders who feel obligated to sustain politically defensive and colonistic models invented for a centuries old world that bears no resemblances to today's world.

Many of today's global leaders and their advisors have no road maps for a world of unprecedented interdependence and change that make certain and durable lines of allies and enemies less viable.

Every year, fewer issues exist within the boundaries of any single country and defy any single country's interventions.

The old decision maker culture of politics promotes a culture of suspicion and separateness. As old adage goes, if you want to control people, you must divide them.

When people move away from these old cultures to new cultures of engagement, they lose interest in borders. They understand that removing borders unleashes the potentials of engagement.

Engaged people see that people who share problems wisely share solutions.

Many problems today exist without borders. These include problems of well-being and homelessness, immigration and civil wars, social unrest and upheavals, human and ecological rights, education and employment.

Every city has these and none can design new futures alone or in nationalistic competition. It will take a global parliament of engaged connected citizens to solve these.

These have no boundaries. They resist any attempts at solutions that have borders whether political, economic or cultural in nature. They require engagement without limits.

They require new chemistries of talents. They require the improbable networks of engaged engineers and scientists, dreamers and doers, poets and artisans, teachers and change agents.

20. Narratives trump numbers

Engagement manifests in the most obvious and palpable ways.

As people become more engaged, look for more people to start up new education options, workplaces and networks within communities. Look for students self-organizing their own learning in preparation for and reinvention of their careers.

Parents will form kibbutzes and networks of home, library and community based schools. Teachers, learning specialists, therapists and advisors will collaborate to provide facilitation and resources.

Employees will start firms within firms, popups and startups. Organizations will empower people as intrapreneurs. Non-profits and funders will become more sustainable by funding people to launch revenue generating enterprises that fund the unfundable.

People in communities will form networks in the commons to pool gardens and farms, emergency loans and shared talents, tools and technologies.

They will teach each other to create together what they previously could only consume. Equipped with new technologies people move from their status as consumers to co-creators, collaborators and contributors.

All of these efforts will produce stories, narratives of progress, courage, learning and success. These narratives will have more power to inspire more than any numbers could make possible. Stories move people into engagement far more quickly and sustainably than statistics.

Engagement as inquiry and listening

The new questions

When we think about new ways of engaging people where they learn, work and live, we take on the challenge of inventing approaches never before imagined in contexts of disengagement.

Facilitation works from new questions. These questions intend to provoke new considerations and possibilities for engagement across contexts. They have the power to look more deeply into how we can invent new ways of designing and facilitating engagement.

These provocative questions have the power to invite people into new conversations that create new kinds of capacity. We can take engagement in these contexts to new levels by introducing these kinds of questions in new conversations. Consider a few dozen questions that get people thinking in new and amazing ways. Invent others.

Education

Why would we have students memorize anything they have instant access to through their phone and will mostly forget? What if we evaluated speed and relevance of access as more important success metrics than memorization? If students did less memorization, would they have more time to learn higher level skills like synthesis, creativity and collaboration?

What could students learn through doing work on actual community relevant projects and internships? How would students contribute more to their communities if they learned empathy through their education because their learning occurred in the context of actual service projects?

Should students learn how to locate, qualify and use their own learning questions and resources? How important do we expect these competencies to be in the future of work and citizenship? What would student motivation for learning look like if student learning actually related directly to their natural and evolving interests and passions?

Could students teach in the afternoon what they learn in the morning as homework practice? How would learners gain from having more positive relationships with more senior learners and alumni?

What character habits will students need for multiple careers in Information Age work? What should we consider the most portable skillsets students can develop? Why might new skills be more important than new knowledge?

Organizations

Could people learn to listen deeply enough to their markets to identify successful growth strategies? Could we develop people working daily in their markets to use their experiences to do research for the creation of strategies?

Could people in work groups interact and get things done through their own co-authored agreements? How would people interact differently if how they worked together was something they co-defined together? How would working from the same page impact people's individual and collective productivity?

Why would we expect that leaders could know more than their people? With easy and real time access to information, could people know as much as or more than their leaders?

Could people learn to make decisions their leaders have tended to make? Could we liberate technology so people could make any decision their leaders used to make? What if we redefined leaders as people who deliver unique kinds of expert value to people? How would leaders behave if they didn't define leadership as one served by others and instead as one who serves others?

Why should we trust that a single discipline would be smarter than a multi-disciplinary team? How do disciplinary silos disable problem solving and decision making? What kinds of problems would we best address across disciplines? Why do the best design firms include multiple disciplines on every project?

Communities

Could people collectively know more than their officials and leaders? What decisions could people crowdsource if they collectively shared more knowledge than any of their leaders could individually know?

How could college and graduate students keep more up to date on expert knowledge than any of their public leaders?

What problems and issues cannot be resolved through individual or competitive efforts within and across communities? What have fragmented or competitive organizations tried to solve and change and haven't because they keep coming from this framework? What new improbable collaborations could bring about progress that would benefit the whole?

What least engaged talents, spaces and resources exist in the community? What if they were more engaged? What new opportunities might be possible? Who could benefit from engaging these more?

Could people share and barter instead of purchase what they only occasionally need? How would local barter economies advantage people with least resources and opportunities? How could local businesses collaborate to explicitly help each other market, grow and succeed?

What kinds of regular events and gatherings could facilitate people dreaming and doing together? What if every consumer event was designed so people could better know each other, share with each other and connect to each other?

Engagement as listening

Listening lives at the core of engagement. When people engage, they listen on three levels. They listen to their questions, to each other and to their world.

Facilitation makes listening easier. It takes people beyond their assumptions, expectations and positions.

When people listen more, they learn more, contribute more and connect more. They transcend the small spaces of their knowns to discover the vast expanse of new possibilities.

All five core practices of facilitation - noticing, nurturing, knitting, noodling and nudging - aim at helping people listen more widely and deeply. Listening empowers people to discover, dream and do in new ways.

Listening to our questions

Everyone has questions because we live with a continuous sense of an intrinsically unknowable future. Our questions represent our unknowns, concerns and interests. Everyone arrives at class, work and their community with questions.

Listening to our questions begins with pondering what we don't know, what we're concerned about and what we're interested in. Whatever questions we have at any point in time, with experience they will change.

People today self-guide their own learning portfolios in any subject or skill domain using online and local sources. Some benefit from coaches, mentors or advisors.

At any age, people gain more learning than they would otherwise get in formal schools or work training programs. Listening to the evolution of their questions inspires the whole process.

As facilitators, we make this process easier and faster. We help them give shape to the most relevant, actionable and productive questions possible.

We do this with individuals and groups. We simply ask people what questions come to mind relative to whatever they strive to achieve. The more people listen to their questions, the more empowered they act in any engagement opportunity.

Listening to each other

Engagement happens best in collaboration. Listening to each other makes collaboration possible.

When we feel heard, we engage more of our gifts for our good and the good of the commons. We give each other the benefit of our doubts. We connect more dots. Our differences enrich rather than threaten our shared capacity for the creative and innovative.

Listening makes trust more possible. Only in environments of trust do people engage their gifts, try something new, venture beyond their assumptions to new stories.

Facilitation makes peer listening easier. We help people make inquiry the core of listening. We help them stay curious about the truth of each other's experience. We offer other, often better, questions for better listening.

Listening to the world

The world now teems with the previously unimaginable and impossible. Locally and virtually, people generously share what was once exclusive to the domain of experts, authorities and publishers. Sharing economies flourish.

Videos, articles and courses offer anything you can imagine and far beyond anything you can imagine. Coaches, mentors and peer companions make mastery of anything possible. Listening to our world unlocks doors, widens windows and empowers passions.

Facilitation connects people to sources one click and conversation away.

Listening shapes engagement. Our most profound impact on groups seeking engagement comes from our ability to help people listen in new ways to their questions, each other and their world.

Facilitator as designer

The power of design

Facilitators design engagement. Skillful facilitation of engagement begins with good design.

When I scan through my portfolio of successful engagement stories, three core elements of design stand out: the invitation, the experiences and the space.

The invitation

The invitation frames the initial intention of engagement. We can describe intentions in very general and ambiguous terms.

We can describe them in very detailed terms. The best invitations welcome people with new questions to which they don't have easy answers.

I find it more effective to frame anything we would call a vision, charge, goal or objective as a question for inviting engagement.

Good invitations have three significant characteristics.

They spark interest. They evoke in people a feeling that the focus of the invitation personally matters to them, their interests, pain or passion.

They represent something new. They come across as a call to something new to learn, accomplish, initiate or complete.

They express clear asks. They tell people what we invite them to do in the process.

The experience

To a large extent, the most significant value we deliver to groups as facilitators involves creating and co-creating with them new experiences that help them more easily do whatever they're trying to do.

We use carefully and creatively crafted questions, suggestions and stories to create new experiences within a group.

New experiences include a group working together to learn, try, share, decide, organize or achieve something new. The most engaging experiences produce some form of actual value for others rather than simulations.

We decide whether we want to give people a recipe to follow or make up their own way. In every case, the group discovers they can do something they have never done together before.

In a well-designed experience, we see everyone involved. We see people making good use of resources within and outside the group in real time. We see people engaging each other's strengths throughout.

The space

Groups work together in local and virtual spaces. Local spaces can take the form of dedicated or shared rooms and venues. Virtual spaces can include shared web sites and pages, apps, video and phone conferencing and messaging.

We use and shape spaces that facilitate comfortable working together and posting work together.

In local spaces, flexible setups allow for improvisational configurations of people, resources and work. In virtual spaces, everything needs to be very accessible and intuitively useful. We design for zero confusions or frustrations.

Posting spaces remain vital. We make sure everything any group generates gets posted and archived somewhere where everyone has easy and instant access.

Most importantly and whenever possible, we get everyone posting their own contributions in their own words, visuals or other media. Posting stimulates more ideas and more ideas lead to better ideas.

The test of good design includes how much people can access through a simple smart phone.

We capture outcomes on sticky notes, flip charts, mind maps, story boards and canvases, in audio and video clips, on blogs and free shared editable documents.

This allows anyone new to the group to have instant inclusion into the group's work and reliable group memory without which progress remains difficult.

Liberating structures

When we facilitate people in their learning, working and living contexts, we don't just ask people what they think. We don't just ask for their ideas or feedback. We don't open the floor to air what everyone has to say. We keep everything continuously focused and productive.

We stay continuously engaged designing and using liberating structures.

In the earlier parts of my career as facilitator, I used successful structures already available. I used models like Problem-based learning, Mindmapping, Open Space Technology, World Cafe, Appreciative inquiry, Lean and Agile Project Management. Each model gives people very specific structures that engage their taking and sharing responsibility for their experience.

Over the decades, I adapted these, combining them in interesting and effective ways. I continue to innovate dozens of other models, sometimes on the spot because a new situation calls for it. In each case, my intention focuses on helping people discover and do something new together.

People and groups less experienced with engagement need far more structure than those with more experience. We assess a group's fluency in engagement by observing what they do naturally in the absence of a decision maker's direction.

We know when a group needs well-crafted structure. They flounder and fragment. People dominate and disappear.

In any case, we design just the right structures to get and keep people moving forward together with intelligence, intuition and inspiration. We have no certainty about the value of any structure until we see it perform real time in a group. We remain continuously attentive and improvisational throughout.

In the ultimate test of good design, we see, hear and feel people coming alive. We observe it in their physical energy, the quality of their conversations, the dynamics among them when they're on their own and the stories that emerge from their efforts together.

Designing courses and workshops

In the old decision maker model of courses and workshops, the sage on the stage and their administrator surrogates dictate the boundaries of what people will learn, when and how. People participate in consumption and compliance of what decision makers impose.

The old model was predicated on the presumption that learners could not possibly know or discover on their own what would best serve their interests, passions and future applicational contexts.

These suppositions lose relevance and power in an era where we can skillfully facilitate learners to discover the right questions and resources for any learning journey.

We can help them learn how to interview people in actual applicational contexts to discover for themselves what's really useful. This becomes an especially critical meta-skill in a world of constantly shifting competency and opportunity requirements.

In the real world, learners will not be handed carefully selected lectures and materials to accompany each problem they encounter. They will not succeed simply on what they know but on how well they could use what they could know or access.

In the most radical departure from the decision maker model, we work from the learner's individual and shared questions relevant to the scope and focus of the invitation.

We guide them to new resources they find and experiences they use to generate new learning and new questions. The more experiential the learning, the better. They feel they own their experience. We simply hold the space for that.

These principles apply to all school learning from pre-school through post-graduate contexts. Any subject or topic can become a source of engaged design where learners learn how to locate, curate and use any available resources inside and outside any walls in their learning spaces.

Through the course of my decades teaching graduate and post-graduate students, they typically credited my status as highest evaluated faculty as my commitment to question based, self-organized learning.

To assess success, people demonstrate new learning and the new and often better questions they take away from their learning. Passion for more learning and doing as an outcome becomes a key marker when we determine our success as facilitators.

Designing work groups and organizations

We can understand organizations as nested networks of groups. Things go well when people engage within and between groups.

On our side as facilitators, people in groups have all the basic skills they need to decide how best to work together and get things done. They only need facilitation to make this possible on a regular basis.
Facilitating engagement within and between any groups in organizations includes three elements: guiding the group in identifying what matters, forming agreements on how

things work relative to what matters and testing and improving agreements in practice.

We ask people what matters to them when it comes to working as a group. We work on one area at a time, forming the best possible agreements on how things would best work for most people. We make exceptions when they make sense to everyone.

Then we have people test out each agreement for a time to assess and tweak for implementation. We do this on a regular basis and have people share success stories. It builds an agile culture of trust, alignment and engagement.

We can do this with work, project and leadership groups. We can facilitate working by agreement across functions and in partnerships with key customers, clients, suppliers and value networks.

Designing community events and collaborations

I cannot count the stories I've heard over the years featuring people coming together in communities where natural disasters have disabled their government officials during the critical windows of recovery opportunities.

People naturally self-organize what decision makers only deliberate into stuckness. When given the opportunity, and without top down vision, mission and value statements, people know how to make the impossible possible. They engage with care, courage, alignment and incredible attention to detail.

Several experiences engage people in communities. Three design elements supporting a wide variety of community engagement include storytelling, learning and agile planning.

We bring people together in circles to tell success stories in the community that enrich the community's faith in itself. We invite them to also share their stories of what they would love to see possible in their communities.

We help people discover anything that could help them realize the stories they would love to see possible. New discoveries of learning inspire, energize and inform people's efforts. People move forward together at the speed of their questions and at the depth of their learning together.

In agile planning, we achieve the smallest versions of any kinds of dreams we have, working in increments of two weeks at a time. We engage whatever gifts we have at the table and invite new gifts whenever it makes sense. Each small achievement builds the group's confidence, learning and resources. We continuously adapt our plan when necessary.

Differences make a difference

As designers of engagement, we pay attention throughout any process to how people engage each other's differences. The better a group leverages its differences, the more differences the group makes.

Groups have all kinds of differences. Each person has a somewhat to very different chemistry of gifts, ways of seeing the world and networks of people they bring to the table.

Thriving groups treat differences as opportunities. Stuck groups treat differences as problems.

People do worse together in groups where they do not appreciate differences. Where differences become sources of division, groups divide into factions and cliques. Divisiveness makes collaboration and anything new less possible. People actually get little done together.

That's why we must as facilitators continuously design ways for people to discover how differences have a unique power similarities do not.

As facilitators, we design conversations that help people know, appreciate and engage everyone's differences. We carefully craft sequences of questions that invite people to consider how any different gifts, perspectives or connections could benefit whatever the group strives to do.

We connect people in the group to new people and resources outside the group that add value to their efforts. We leverage the use of personal storytelling to build the kind of trust that makes people more comfortable with people unlike themselves.

We design conversations that help people discover more of what they have in common including common stories, likes, dislikes, struggles and dreams.

Groups that love their differences also love the amazing grace of serendipity because uncertainty and unfamiliarity open space for new possibilities.

Much of our work as designers of engagement involves helping people leverage uncertainty as opportunity for empowerment, creativity and new connections. Groups transcend small agendas, self-interest and fear when they learn to love differences.

Practice activities

The practice workbook

In this workbook section, you can choose from any of the 60 practice activities organized by the 5 core dimensions of facilitation.

Before you get into using the practice activities here, start by reading through them and identifying those you feel you're already doing fairly well. Starting with a sense of your strengths energizes you for the work of developing more facility with others.

Work on a few at a time. You can start by creating a list of practice activities you want to spend time with, sequencing them in an agile order that makes sense to your interests in growing your facilitation craft.

You can start with ones that you believe will have the greatest immediate benefit to whatever facilitating you're currently doing. The activities here provide studio practice to strengthen and complement the practice you do live with groups.

Change the order of skillsets you're working on any time it makes sense based on the facilitation opportunities you're engaged in.

If you're currently facilitating multiple groups, you can select one or two things to work on with each group based on their differences in character or contexts.

Each practice has applications in any kind of educational, organizational and community contexts. They work their magic in any course or training, work process or project, event or gathering.

Each practice activity presents a brief view of the facilitation mindset and skillset, followed by an activity for practice.

You can accelerate and deepen your growth by journaling both your practice activities and experiences using these skillsets with people you're facilitating. The practice of journaling has unique power on any learning path.

You can also enrich your learning by sourcing the plethora of articles and videos now available that address any aspects of facilitation and engagement.

In addition, some of my other books outline models and approaches for facilitating engagement, including: *Appreciative Leadership, Instructions From The Cook, The Stories That Connect Us* and *The Agile Planning Field Guide.*

Noticing practices

Knowing a group's character and dynamics in a way that makes it easier to facilitate them

Think about how many things we could know, not know and sense about any group. The more we know about a group, the more opportunities emerge into our view. Knowing comes about through observations, informal conversations and interacting in new ways with people in the group.
Knowing a group better than it knows itself gives us an edge in staying more proactive than reactive.

On the list of things we can discover: people's gifts, personalities, questions, dreams, opportunities, relationships, dynamics, influences, commonalities, differences, shifts and changes.

...
Name 5 things you know for sure about a group, 10 things you don't know and 3 things you intuitively sense about it.

Identifying who in a group has the most potential to help others take risks

Everyone shows up with various tolerances for ambiguity and uncertainty. In every group people interact with relatively more or less enthusiasm for discovering new things beyond their familiarity and comfort zones.

Moving any group into anything new starts with helping the relatively more enthusiastic early adoptors get engaged and lead the way.

...

Design questions you could use to identify a group's discomfort zones and readiness for something new and different.

Assessing the levels of engagement in a group

Noticing the levels and shifts in people's engagement requires us to use all of our senses that feed our intuition. We look at emotional energy expressed in voice tones, peer eye contact, body language, emotional vocabularies, quality of interactions and outcomes of actions.

We attend to signs of people coming alive and fading away, momentum and stuckness so we can support and intervene responsively and proactively. Some of this happens when we check in with people informally while waiting for things to begin or complete.

...

Name some of a group's more obvious signs of engagement and disengagement.

Knowing the kinds of questions that keep groups stuck and productive

Groups become most stuck or productive because of the quality of questions that shape their experience. Questions include their interests, unknowns and concerns. Unless we explicitly identify people's questions, we might never know, which disables our ability to help them move on to more productive questions.

To help groups move in the direction of their most productive questions, we first must know any they might have. If we identify the questions that seem to keep them stuck or distracted, we can help them move onto better ones.

...

Identify the kinds of questions that keep a group stuck and the kinds that could make them productive in whatever they're trying to attempt or achieve.

Assessing for the strengths in a group

Think of a strength as something people enact with
relative competence and something they like or love
doing. Everyone has strengths, even if they spend little
time thinking or talking about them. Facilitation engages
strengths in ways that create new possibilities of learning,
doing and interacting.

As facilitator, we take time to get to know people's unique
and common strengths so we can personally call on them
when we engage people in anything new and meaningful.
The more people become conscious of their strengths, the
more naturally they engage them.

...
Name the dominant and most useful strengths that exist in
a group and think of ways to better know their strengths.

Mapping the group's social network connections

We think of groups as social networks. We discover and
monitor the patterns of connections and disconnections so
we can create new connections and strengthen existing
connections. We facilitate the creation and strengthening
of connections by inviting people to share their
commonalities, gifts and interests.

The quality of individual actions and interactions in a
group often reflects the quality of relationships in the
group. The more positive connections we create and
strengthen in any ways, the better people learn, produce
and collaborate.

...
Map the more obvious patterns of connection and
disconnection within the group and in relationship to
other relevant groups

Intuiting when people do and don't feel heard

People get engaged to the degree they feel heard by others in the group. People who don't feel heard disengage in any numbers of passive and disruptive ways, checking or acting out. In facilitation, we pause interactions to make sure people feel heard.

We do whatever we can to help people unheard give voice to their experience in ways that others accurately receive it. We help people articulate and ask better questions for clarification.

...

Describe who in a group you think feels most and least heard by others and what you could do to bring about more possibilities of people feeling heard.

Knowing which areas of our own subject matter expertise has value to the group's questions

When the group wants subject matter expertise that we have, we offer it in any media that works. We always put a premium on helping them self-organize their own discovery of something we could otherwise simply hand to them. Discovered learning always remains 8-10 times more sustainable and useful than delivered learning.

Our readiness to facilitate just-in-time learning, in contrast to just-in-case learning, requires vigilance and responsiveness to people's unpredictable questions as soon as they emerge.

...

Name areas of your own subject matter expertise that might be relevant, useful and received by a group.

Observing where the group's attention flows

Groups move in the direction of their attention. We discover what a group pays attention to in relationship to themselves, each other and their world and to past, present and future. The focus of their attention shows up in what they talk about.

We use questions to get people focused on something new that can help them do whatever they're trying to do. When a group's focus of attention changes, new possibilities appear.

...
Describe what you think a group already does and doesn't pay attention to and craft questions that could help them pay more attention to something new.

Knowing what kinds of new resources the group thinks they have access to

Groups disable their potentials most when they rely too dominantly on their own resources or those of the decision makers in their world. This problem was intractable in past eras where access otherwise was far beyond any group's media or means.

In the Information Age, many people have affordable access to the world's knowledge and real time information through a browser in the palm of their hand. They also live in networks that position them less than a dozen steps from many of the 7 billion people on the planet.

Facilitation connects people to new resources they never imagined existed.

...

Identify new outside resources a group would benefit from discovering and using.

Paying attention to people receptive and reluctant to offer and ask for help

In every group, individuals get stuck and don't ask for help. People would offer help if they knew it was needed. Many people suffer from habits of resisting asking for help or offering help when it isn't explicitly requested.

We pay attention to anyone who gets stuck in any way. We quickly connect them with someone who can help, whether help exists ten feet or ten time zones away. As facilitator, we act as the last resort.

...

Identify who in a group asks for help, offers help, does neither and should, and would give help if asked.

Identifying who in a group we can engage to help facilitate

Facilitation builds a group's capacity to facilitate itself. This means cultivating facilitation skillsets with people in the group who show interest in and promise for it. We keep our intuition tuned to identify these people.

We look for signs of facilitation strengths and interests. We invite people with these to take over for us at times and carefully notice where they need encouragement and affirmation.

...
Identify who in a group shows the most promise and interest in helping to facilitate anything the group does.

Nurturing practices

Helping people feel respected for their stories, beliefs and feelings

People get engaged in a group to the degree they feel supported by others in the group. People feel supported when they feel that others validate the truth of their experience - their stories, beliefs and feelings.

We model and invite validation. In validation, we might or might not agree or identify with another's experience. We simply and honestly affirm that we understand how real it feels for them.

...

Identify stories, beliefs and feelings in a group that get most and least validated by people in the group and think of ways to more explicitly validate people's experience.

Making everyone feel a sense of belonging in the group

We do whatever we can to create a space of hospitality where people feel a sense of belonging. We model and invite inclusion when people feel left out or unacknowledged.

We also make it easier for people to feel valuable to the group by reminding the group to engage people's gifts in any ways they can. Feeling valuable doesn't require that people share their gifts, they only have to be asked.

...

Craft options to make it more possible for people to feel welcome in a group.

Keeping your energy positive as facilitator

Facilitation makes our energy contagious. When we keep
our energy positive, we have more credibility and
influence. Positive energy also makes us less sensitive to
any kind of negative energy in the group.

We need to develop habits that keep our energy positive
when we facilitate groups. These can be habits of health,
inspiration and focus.

...

Make a commitment to start or strengthen some habit that
will help keep your energy positive in a group.

Acting with transparency, credibility and trustworthiness

How people in the group feel about us gives us our power as facilitator. We do not rely on authority as a surrogate to authenticity. People empower us to facilitate them when they feel good about us. Whatever we do to practice transparency, credibility and trustworthiness makes it easier for people to empower us as facilitator.

Doing this happens immediately and continuously as we work with any group. We make and keep small promises. We don't allow people to guess what we're about or after. We share our own stories that speak to our credibility.

...

Describe what it might mean for you to strengthen your transparency, credibility and trustworthiness in a group.

Helping people ask good questions of each other in the group

When people engage well, they show interest in each other. An engaged group becomes an interesting group. People feel as interesting as they act interested.

We help people develop the habit of asking questions to each other that help them act with creativity, compassion, collaboration and courage. We model and invite questions that express interest in what people aren't yet saying but our intuition suggests they have to share.

...

Craft questions that could help people express more interest in each other's perspectives and experiences.

Getting groups to base their interactions and
actions on group agreements

Aligned groups move faster and smarter together. Any
agreements they make on how they work and interact
together form alignment. We help them craft and test new
agreements that matter to the group.

Agreements can be about anything. They can address how
the group communicates, learns, plans, shares resources,
gets things done, addresses issues and opportunities.

We encourage the group to make and keep agreements
most people can support. Until a group creates and keeps
agreements, things happen by dictate, default or the
whims of dominant personalities.

...
List new categories of agreements a group could create
that could build and strengthen alignment.

Inviting people to experiment and improvise for new learning

Groups need permission to experiment with new ways of learning, working and interacting together. They need to change course whenever it makes sense. Any way that isn't working needs to be changed.

We encourage necessary failure for the sake of learning and improvising. We lower risks by encouraging fast failure at small scales. We invite people to view every single thing they attempt and do as an experiment.

...

Identify ways you could give a group permission for new experiments and improvisations.

Creating an environment where the group can feel confident in itself as a group

Confident groups want more from themselves and their world. They dream bigger. When groups have confidence in themselves as a group, they become unstoppable.

Groups that regularly acknowledge their gifts and progress act with confidence. Confidence gives them a sense of persistence in the face of challenges and agility in the face of change.

...
Name 3 ways to help a group feel more confident in itself as a group.

Showing genuine care as facilitator for people in the group

Engaged people care for each other. We create an environment of caring with our own genuine caring. People don't care how much we know until they know how much we care. We only have authentic influence in a group that believes we genuinely care about their collective success and personal well-being.

Genuine caring takes many forms. We show interest in what people personally celebrate and struggle with. We offer our greatest gift of time when people need help with something. We followup with something that shows we have them in mind even when we're remote.

...

Describe simple ways you can show sincere personal care and concern to people in a group.

Engaging different personalities at the right time

Just as no kitchen has bad ingredients, no group has bad people. We look at different personalities as different gifts to engage at different times rather than different problems to fix. People feel valued. Timing makes the difference.

We pay attention to when we can best engage which differences. When the group needs to get realistic, we engage the researchers. When they need new options, we engage the idea people. When they need to anticipate problems, we engage the worriers. When the group needs to get moving, we engage the action people.

...

Name 3 ways to engage the right gifts in a group at the right time.

Helping people respond to each other's new ideas in ways that help them grow

Creativity thrives in an environment where people feel like their ideas can grow. Ideas grow when people initially respond with what they like about an idea rather than how they can dismiss or disable it.

We invite this kind of appreciative critique in any new idea conversation. People cling to their ideas and inhibit new ones to the degree they feel like they have to defend them against attack or apathy. We free people up to new possibilities by simply inviting what's good about any idea that comes up.

...
Describe what kinds of questions could get a group helping people's new ideas grow

Inviting people to opt into whatever the group does rather than feel coerced into it

Coercion prevents engagement. When people feel coerced into anything, they resist engagement. Coercion strips people of their ability to choose. When people lose choice, they lose interest and act unengaged.

We always give people the choice to participate or not in anything the group does. We never allow the oxymoron of coerced engagement because only authentic engagement works. When people feel free to not participate, they feel most free to participate.

...

Describe when and how you could make it more clear to people they have a choice to participate or not.

Knitting practices

Organizing any scope of work into small groups

Research continues to support the idea that when it comes to people working together in groups, smart works small. 4-5 people make up optimal groups whether their purpose focuses on dialogue, planning, decision making, learning or work.

We can leverage the power of connected small groups to make progress on the largest projects. This requires two elements: chunking anything down into ingredient pieces and creating intersecting and nested circles of groups that engage gifts, commonalities and complements.

...

Design different ways to cluster people in a group to tackle work in small groups of two or more.

Designing spaces for people to collaborate at any time

The overwhelming research indicates that the vast majority of people do their best learning and thinking outside formal contexts of meetings and courses. The design of most meetings and courses actually disable creativity and discovery.

As facilitators, we design collaborative spaces that engage the best in people for learning and thinking. We create physical walls and web pages offering ongoing spaces for contributing and collaborating. We use meetings to organize rather than do work that could be done outside meetings.

...

Design physical and online visual environments where people can collaborate outside meetings or classes.

Weaving new meaningful connections between and among people in a network

When people feel connected, they do better. We connect people by inviting them to share their questions, dreams, gifts, stories and learning. People in groups have much to offer each other. Their collaborations extend value beyond what any single decision maker could ever offer.

We look for and improvise any opportunity or excuse to get people doing together anything they might try doing disconnected on their own.

...

Name 5 ways to connect people in new ways in a group.

Leveraging storytelling to build new and stronger relationships

Nothing connects people more significantly than the stories they can personally relate and resonate with. Nothing bonds people more than sharing narratives of common interest and empathy.

We can invite people to tell stories of their learning experiences, their success and disappointment experiences, their everyday experiences of struggle and gratitude.

...
Identify the kinds of stories that would help people form new bonds of shared experience or identity.

Helping groups make better and faster decisions together

Engaged people make timely and smart decisions together. We help them use all available resources to make good decisions.

We encourage them to set timeframes for all decisions even if they have to adjust them. We don't take decisions away from them even when we're tempted to think we know better. We help them base their process on their ever-evolving questions.

We encourage groups to have a few do the research all will then use to make timely decisions that work.

...

Identify decisions a group should and could start making together.

Keeping introverts and extroverts balanced in engagement

Every group has extroverts and introverts, people who think by talking and others who think by listening. Facilitation gets talkers listening and listeners talking. We do this by asking different questions of each so talking and listening stays balanced.

Groups with balanced listening and talking act smarter together. We actually decrease the collective intelligence, intuition, and innovation in a group when we encourage or allow people to divide into two classes of talkers and listeners.

..

Name 3 ways to balance conversations between those who tend to be more extroverted and introverted in a group.

Engaging people from outside the group to add complementary value to its efforts

Outside every group lives an infinite space of possibilities. We live on a planet abundant with people who know how to do anything and can teach others what they know. Every school, organization and community has people who have gifts no one invites them to share.

As facilitators we connect people in our groups to people outside our groups. We make these kinds of introductions happen. We inspire people to remain continuously curious about who they might connect with next.

...

Name 5 people outside a group who could add different kinds of value to the group.

Getting people in a group teaching each other what they know

People in groups have all kinds of learning they can share with each other. Shared learning becomes more sustainable for the one who shares. For many reasons, peer-to-peer learning proves more effective and efficient than expert instructed learning.

Any opportunity that presents itself, we connect people in peer learning. Everyone wins because learners don't have to figure everything out themselves and people who teach master their learning more in the process. Ultimately we want people to engage each other naturally in this.

...

Think of ways people could teach each other something they have learned, know or can do.

Engaging decision makers to interact as peers with the group

Most groups have people designated as in charge. With various levels of authority and incentives, they think their job exists to assume more responsibility for the group than the group assumes.

This sets up an obligation that people should treat their relationship with the person in charge as more important than their relationships with the rest of the group.

We liberate people from this constraint by inviting the person in charge to engage in the group as a peer. We especially engage anything of unique value they have to offer the group. We also help them engage instead as facilitator whenever it makes sense.

...

Think of ways you can engage decision makers as peers in contributing what they uniquely bring to the table.

Connecting one group to others for mutual gain

Every group has dreams it can only achieve in collaboration with other groups. To connect these groups, we first look for people in each group already naturally connected in positive ways. We invite them to explore ways to connect both groups in efforts of mutual benefit.

We engage them as connectors to create more natural connections of help and value exchange between and among the groups. This creates relationships across groups that makes new collaborations more possible for things that no group has the resources to achieve alone.

...

Identify people across groups who could make new connections to support possible new collaborations.

Helping people move from differences to commonalities

For a variety of reasons, groups struggle with tensions between differences. The group gets stuck in factions and conflict. It can get to a point where people believe they have little or nothing in common.

Facilitation moves people beyond the illusion of only-differences. We engage people in discovering their similar and complementary gifts, questions, concerns, dreams and stories.

...

Identify questions you could use to help a group become more aware of similarities and complements in the group.

Getting the connectors in a group introducing and connecting people not yet connected

Every group has natural connectors. These people enjoy connecting people. They eagerly make sure people get introduced. They look to include people who seem somewhat to very isolated or disconnected from others.

They connect people through any media and locations available. They tend to have higher levels of likeability, empathy and credibility.

As facilitators, we support them in any ways we can to do their connecting within groups and between and among groups. We might point out connection opportunities and offer to help initiate and grow new connections.

...

Create 3-5 questions you could use to help people engage more as connectors in a group

Noodling practices

Getting a group to generate increasingly valuable ideas and options

When it comes to new ideas and questions, quantity leads to quality. More ideas and questions lead to better ideas and questions. Our first ideas and questions inspire others that grow in value.

When a group needs to generate better questions and ideas, we keep asking new questions to inspire and provoke new iterations of options, variations and possibilities. We also give people relaxed time for new ones to emerge which typically happens when they don't try to think about new ideas.

...

Create as many different kinds of questions as you can to get people generating more ideas or questions related to something they're working on.

Helping people work collaboratively on new ideas and options

When people generate a new idea, others can react to it in any number of ways. They can act as though they didn't hear the idea. They can try to discredit the idea with push back, criticisms or complaints.

People can also respond in ways that help ideas grow into new and better versions and variations. We facilitate this by asking three questions: What could you add to make this idea even better? (and); How do you see this working? (so); What else could achieve the same purposes? (else).

...

Identify some opportunities when you could introduce these three questions in a group.

Inviting people to use empathy to create new kinds of value

People feel most powerfully engaged when they think of new ways to create value for other people that solves real problems or helps realize their dreams. This practice of empathy characterizes the heart of the entrepreneurial mindset. It catalyzes better learning, performance and participation in any context.

We create any opportunity we can to help people identify new kinds of value they could produce for people in their world. We use these opportunity spaces as contexts to focus and energize all kinds of new research, learning, inventing, prototyping, experimenting and improvising.

...

Identify 4-5 questions that could get people identifying new ways to connect what they're learning or doing to what might have actual value to others outside the group.

Inviting people to use improvisation for continuous improvement in what they're doing

Continuous improvement engages people in unique and valuable ways. Every group has things it does that represent opportunities for improvement. This means making something faster, better, cheaper or easier.

We get the group experimenting with different ways to improve anything about their world.

We guide them in deciding what kinds of experiments to run, where and how long to run them and how to measure the gains and costs. We create an environment where people consider experimenting business as usual in whatever they're striving to do.

...
Identify an experiment the group can do and describe your suggestions for how it gets designed.

Visualizing people's contributions to spark new possibilities and organize work

Unless ideas become visible, they get lost in space and lose their ability to spark new options, variations and combinations. We make sure people post every contribution for everyone to access on a physical wall, virtual wall or both.

We make sure everyone writes out their own ideas for accuracy, completeness and a sense of personal authorship. No one records other people's contributions. The act of writing and visualizing ideas neurologically stimulates more ideas than simply speaking them.

...
Decide on the ways you could facilitate this in an upcoming group meeting or learning event.

Giving people permission and support to be
inspired by their dreams

Engaged people dream. They use the passion of their
dreams to shape what they discover, achieve and share
where they learn, work and live. Most people need
guidance in discovering and articulating their dreams.

We help people connect the dots of their dreams with
whatever they're currently doing.

We do this with simple questions. What would you love to
see possible in your life and world? What's the impossible
you would love to see possible? What would be a wow
here? What would surprise people in positive ways?

We encourage people to see dreams not as locations they
must achieve in an unknowable future but powerful lenses
that reveal new possibilities in the present.

...
Describe how inviting people's dreams could be the basis
for anything new they learn, do or share.

Guiding people to move from dreaming to doing

Action in the present gives dreams their power. Dreams go unrealized unless we translate them into actions and projects we invent in the present. We guide people in the creative process of inventing small acts that could help realize their dream in any ways.

Small acts utilize what we have and can do to realize any aspects or variations on our dreams.

...

Think of small acts that could help realize any dreams people have in a group.

Helping the group stimulate new ideas through their technologies

We live in a limitless world of discovery through our technologies. Websites, blogs, videos, online publications, and social media hold unpredictable treasures when it comes to sparking new ideas and alternatives.

In facilitation we redirect any group trying to get inspired through circular discussion to their virtual resources.

This applies equally to new ideas for learning, working and living.

...

Identify the kinds of new learning that people could gain through online sources and their social and professional networks.

Inviting people from outside the group to add new perspectives, resources and gifts

Creativity happens when we make unplanned new connections between things that already exist. The more exposure people have to what's new and unfamiliar, the greater chances they have of stumbling on new insights.

We take every opportunity to create this kind of environment.

We invite people to dialogue in person or virtually with the group who can offer exposure to whole new vistas. We invite people with inspiring stories, poetry, inventions, art, craft or scientific expertise in anything any group pursues.

...

Name 3 people you could invite to dialogue with a group to expose them to new possibilities and perspectives relative to whatever they're up to.

Empowering people with design thinking

Engaged people think like designers. They see all problems as design problems.

Whatever a group tries to do, we invite them to look at their efforts as a design opportunity. We ask them how they would go about designing what they're after.

We invite them to play with different optional approaches. We have them experiment with ways that seem most promising. This empowers them to take responsibility for their process in any context.

...

Craft questions that could engage people in taking a design mindset to whatever they're working on.

Creating a lighthearted environment that makes creativity more fluid

The research indicates that during the course of our formal education, our engagement in creativity follows the same decline as our engagement in play. By the time we complete our formal education, we have lost over 90% of our fluency with creativity.

The good news from the neurosciences indicates that we can reawaken our capacity for creativity at any point in our life through play. Play can take the form of fun, spontaneity, humor and informality. We leverage the ha-ha to spark the ah-ha in any spaces we can create.

...

Name a few ways you can lighten up the spirit of a group in anything they attempt to do.

Moving groups from either-or to both-and
thinking by leveraging the power of polarities

All groups get stuck. They run into problems that quickly
resist the easy answers from the past.

Groups stay stuck by turning any question into an either-or
question. The debate about which prevents productive
discovery and creativity.

Creativity thrives when the group turns any question into a
both-and question. The dialogue about how we might be
able to achieve even opposite considerations has amazing
power to spark richer and more sustainable options.

When groups get stuck in either-or debates, we shift the
conversation to the dialogue on both-and. When the
group divides into conflicts over opposites, we help them
see that they wisely consider both intentions for a viable
solution to emerge.

...
Identify the either-or questions a group could get stuck on
and what questions could move them to both-and.

Nudging practices

Moving the unknown from a source of fear to opportunity

Anytime we ask people to enter new territories of engagement, they respond along a continuum between interest and intimidation, depending on how much control they feel they need in their life and world. Intimidation prevents engagement.

However people respond to new challenges, they move forward by translating new uncertainties into new actionable questions that empower them. Actionable questions require some kinds of research, decision or experiments to address.

...

Describe ways you could help people translate the uncertainties of their unknowns, concerns and interests into new actionable questions.

.

Using stories to inspire people to new spaces of possibility

As facilitators, we continuously grow and curate our portfolio of good stories that inspire people into new levels of enthusiasm, optimism, hope and courage. Good stories move people from division and discouragement to engagement.

Whether we collect our stories or other people's stories, a well-told story at the right time infuses people with positive energy that supports the buoyancy of their engagement.

Good stories have specific structures that feature real characters who come through problems better than before. People stay engaged when their spirits come to life. Good storytelling makes this possible.

...

Identify good stories you could use to inspire people in a group.

Guiding people in questioning their own inaccurate beliefs and assumptions

Anytime people encounter a new challenge, they have some kinds of inaccurate assumptions and beliefs about it. People do this with a new learning opportunity, problem, project or challenge.

We surface these and offer people questions that invite them to challenge their own assumptions and beliefs. We use why, how and what-if questions that encourage people to explore the opposite possibilities from what they currently expect.

...

Craft questions you could use to help people question any inaccurate assumptions and beliefs.

Helping people organize together any scope of work

Groups get things done because they approach them in logical sequences of success stories.

A success story represents anything we want or need to see happen. We identify as many as we can, put them in order of how they need to be achieved and assign time stamps indicating when we will complete each story.

We get people doing what relates best to their gifts. We make sure we know how much time people can afford to the process and we utilize all available time wisely.

As we move forward in any effort, change remains a constant. We think of new stories, some stories become irrelevant and the order of stories shifts.

...
Outline how you could help people define, sequence and timeframe their success stories.

Moving people from conversations that keep
them stuck to those that get them moving
forward together in a positive direction

Until people become engaged, negativity represents the
conversational norm. People talk about what they can't
do, don't have and don't want. People bond in the
innocence of their victimhood.

In facilitation we empower people with questions that
shift them from victims to authors of their experience.

We focus them on what they like and want, what they
have and can do with what they have. This shift gives
them permission to take responsibility for their life and
their world instead of outsourcing to others.

...

Identify questions that could help people move from
victimizing to empowering conversations.

Coaching individuals to support their success

People sometimes need individual support. They struggle with something others don't struggle with. They need different kinds of affirmation, resources or refocusing beyond what their peers can offer.

We first make sure they've reached out to peers for any help they might have to offer. Then we provide backup coaching to help them move productively forward.

Many times we ask people to do things they know how to do and need nudging to do in spite of their feelings. This empowers them to engage their strengths in new ways.

Coaching in its simplest form involves four elements: asking people what matters to them, asking them which of their gifts will help make this possible, asking them why they will commit to doing and asking them to reflect on what they learn from their experiences.

...

Identify how coaching individuals in a group would help people succeed.

Moving people from talk to action

Sometimes people get stuck in futile loops of discussion, speculation and debate. They act as if more talk will lead to new possibilities. We intervene to move them into action because no amount of more thinking and talking will lead to anything new.

We use questions to encourage people to instead do some research, start an experiment or project, invite others into the process, take a break to do some reflection or move the conversation to new questions of some kind. These get them moving forward.

...

Name 3 questions that could help people move from talk to action.

Helping groups sustain positive energy for endurance and resiliency

Motivation comes from progress. Celebrating progress of even small steps gives us energy that supports next steps. We take a few minutes on a regular basis to ask people to talk about what they're achieving, learning and discovering. We ask them to talk about what's working and why.

This creates positive energy that gives people endurance and resiliency. Naive beliefs argue that extrinsic incentives and threats have the power to sustain people's energy. In reality they do not. Only celebrating success with stories has this power.

...

Describe how people could use their stories of progress and achievement to celebrate progress and successes.

Helping people focus on their strengths in ways that make their weaknesses less relevant

The old folklore, unsupported by the data, has us believe that we only get better as human beings when we focus on our weaknesses. The research indicates otherwise. We only get better when we focus on our potentials, our gifts of abilities, knowledge, resources, stories, questions and connections.

We succeed in any endeavor precisely to the degree that we engage our gifts. We only engage our gifts when they remain top of mind. Facilitation keeps people focused on their gifts in ways that make their weaknesses irrelevant.

...

Define what it would mean to get people to focus more on their gifts than weaknesses.

Guiding people through facilitation rather than instruction

When we bring more subject matter expertise to the table than the group has, we become tempted to play the ultimate source of knowledge. As efficient as this seems, it prevents engagement.

Instead, we guide people in crafting how they will go after what they need to learn. We let them know what we have to offer and encourage them to discover other sources as well through any media or technology available.

...

Identify when you could feel tempted to tell people what to think and do instead of helping them arrive at this themselves.

Helping groups take on decisions that used to be made for them by decision makers

People engage when they make decisions decision makers made for them. As facilitators, we put our priority on building capacity rather than compliance.

We help people learn to take over decisions that shape their engagement. We do this in steps, first modeling, then having them experiment as collaborators and finally taking over decisions when they can.

...

Identify what you usually decide for a group and outline how you could guide them in taking over and sharing in these decisions over time.

Engaging people's imagination to inspire new positive energy and perspectives

We nudge people into new possibility spaces by inviting them to imagine the best for themselves and their world.

We describe something they would love to see and simply ask them to just imagine that. "Imagine that ..." creates a positive energy resonance that inspires their creativity, courage and connectivity.

The nudge has the power to catalyze a shift. This especially empowers people when they feel frustrated, stressed or isolated. We follow up with questions getting them to consider how they could help bring about any parts of whatever their heart imagines.

...

Identify examples of when asking people to imagine something new might help them shift from stuckness to thriving.

Holding space

I like the idea of facilitation as holding space for engagement.

Holding space means creating a specific kind of energy that makes it easier for a group to do their best together. The word facilitation originates from the Latin, facilis, meaning to make easier.

Holding space means encircling a group with the energy of curiosity, inspiration, resilience, creativity, listening and empathy. When a group resonates with this energy, they become amazing and unstoppable.

Holding space for a group means doing whatever we can to make it easier for people to engage and connect their own and each other's gifts and questions, stories and resources in new ways.

Making things easier can take several forms. Sometimes we show interest, declare permission, express optimism, demonstrate care, encourage initiative, validate intention, share questions, invite gifts and make connections.

Other times, we stay out of the way, wait to be invited, provide a non-anxious presence, validate people by listening without interruption or judgment and encourage people to draw from their inner wisdom and intuition.

Holding space has unique power to draw people in, out and beyond. When we don't hold space, we or anyone in the group dominates it. Dominating space makes it more difficult for a group to take and share responsibility for itself. It decreases the possibilities of engagement.

When we hold space for a group, people listen, inquire, appreciate, play, invite, share, help, join, create, experiment, connect, learn and grow.

The most significant indicator of holding space happens when a group holds space for itself. They unfold the ancient alchemy of shared responsibility. They discover the power of circles.

About the author

Jack Ricchiuto remains best known across the US and globally for his experience as writer and engagement artisan.

Jack's career as engagement artisan began in the 1970's as apprentice with the first generation global leaders of the human potentials movement that would give root to the transformational research and practices of positive psychology.

Over the next three decades, he leveraged this foundation into work across industry and geographic sectors with organizations and communities interested in creating cultures of change through engagement.

Jack's professional writing career started in the early 1990's which has produced over a dozen books, several blogs and contributions to professional print and online publications. His books cover a range of topics including growing edge questions in leadership, innovation, agile planning, the power of narrative, mindfulness, change, and community and network building.

In his groundbreaking work today with organizations, communities, and education, Jack teaches groups how to realize their potential.

As a subject matter expert, Jack has supported organizations, universities, and communities across sectors including NASA, Chrysler, FedEx, Federal Reserve

Bank, Smithers Oasis, US EPA, Red Cross, AT&T, Catholic Charities, Moen, University of North Texas, Cleveland and Detroit schools, University Hospitals, American Greetings, USDA, and leaders from several urban core and rural communities around the world. He acts as the Senior Facilitator for the global Entrepreneurial Learning Initiative in partnership with the Kauffman Foundation.

Jack's books include *Collaborative Creativity, Accidental Conversations, Project Zen, Appreciative Leadership, Mountain Paths, Conscious Becoming, Instructions from the Cook, The Stories that Connect Us, The Enchantment of Casual Origins, The Joy of Thriving, Ordinary Eyes, The Agile Planning Field Guide, Abundant Possibilities* and *The Power Of Circles.*

Jack was among the earliest website, blog, and social media contributors and has been a journalist and subject matter expert to professional magazines, journals and conference speaking events.

Since 1980, Jack has been designing and teaching leadership and professional development workshops and courses with a variety of campus and online undergraduate, graduate, and post-Doc programs including Kent State University, UC Berkeley, and the University of Charleston. He mentors faculty and curriculum designers.

Jack's undergraduate degree in clinical psychology resides from John Carroll University and graduate degree in positive psychology hails from Goddard College, Vermont.

He lives in the Tremont community of urban Cleveland Ohio in the Great Lakes region.

For more about Jack, his writing and work, visit JackRicchiuto.com